Praise for *Moving Miss Peggy*

"Enter softly into these pages, for this most beautiful book will bear you into the very center of life itself and show you all the bittersweet goodness to be found there."
—Phyllis Tickle, compiler, *The Divine Hours*

"This work is a rare gift at a time when dementia and Alzheimer's are increasing in alarming numbers. Benson writes cleanly and honestly. He writes lovingly, yet never with sentimentality. He writes helpfully, yet never with a secret agenda of telling us 'how to.' *Moving Miss Peggy* unfolds as a poignant expression of the ways in which love is able to transform even decline and loss into greater love. A beautiful book."
—Paula D'Arcy, author of *Gift of the Red Bird* and *Waking Up to This Day*

"With each book, Robert Benson nudges open the door to his world a bit further, inviting us inside to meet the people most dear to him. We soon discover our own family members standing in the doorway, our own memories filling the air. In *Moving Miss Peggy*, we learn how we, too, might weather the storm, should the time come. Filled with hope and a wry sense of humor."
—Liz Curtis Higgs, author of *The Girl's Still Got It*

"A gritty, truthful, heartbreaking but ultimately inspiring story."
—Tim Takacs, Certified Elder Law Attorney, Hendersonville, Tennessee

Praise for Robert Benson

"Benson's tone remains down-to-earth, and the analogies he draws hit the mark."
—*The New York Times Book Review*

"As always, Benson's deceptively sneaky storytelling sneaks up on you. His style, a fusion of gentleness, raw truth, and quiet power . . . is put to good use."
—Nikki Grimes, author of *Bronx Masquerade*

"Robert Benson reminds us of what we too often forget—that the ground we walk upon is sacred."
—Frederic and Mary Ann Brussat, coauthors of *Spiritual Literacy* and directors of SpiritualityandPractice.com

Moving Miss Peggy

A Story of Dementia, Courage, and Consolation

ROBERT BENSON

Abingdon Press
NASHVILLE

MOVING MISS PEGGY
A STORY OF DEMENTIA, COURAGE, & CONSOLATION

Copyright © 2013 by Robert Benson

Library of Congress Cataloging-in-Publication Data

Benson, R. (Robert), 1952-
 Moving Miss Peggy : a story of dementia, courage & consolation / Robert Benson.
    pages cm
 ISBN 978-1-4267-4957-5 (hardback with printed dust jacket : alk. paper) 1. Dementia—Patients—Family relationships. 2. Dementia—Patients—Care—Psychological aspects. 3. Aging parents—Care. I. Title.
 RC521.B47 2013
 616.8'3—dc23

                                                        2013006938

13 14 15 16 17 18 19 20 21 22—10 9 8 7 6 5 4 3 2 1

MANUFACTURED IN THE UNITED STATES OF AMERICA

This book is for Miss Peggy, of course,
for her children & all who love her.

It is for Papa—we did our best.

It is for all who face this particular darkness,
& all who love and care for them.

And it is for the Friends of Silence & of the Poor,
whoever & wherever you may be.

There is nothing to remember about her except the good.

—Donna Leon

Contents

ONE

I See the Water   1

TWO

The Legend   15

THREE

A Gathering Up   25

FOUR

A First Gift   37

FIVE

Of Keys and Burdens   47

SIX

Moving Days   59

Contents

SEVEN

The Wizards 71

EIGHT

Pack It Up, Move It Out 85

NINE

Homing In 99

TEN

Small Prices 117

ELEVEN

Stay in Touch 127

TWELVE

Loss and Found 141

THIRTEEN

Going Out Singing 151

Notes and Acknowledgments 161

1

I See the Water

This is the story of moving Miss Peggy to a new place to live, to a new way of life, to a new kind of reality. All of which became necessary because she has begun to live a life colored by a disease called dementia. All of us who love her have begun to live that new life with her. Some of that story is here as well.

Peggy Jean Siler Benson is her name. She will answer to most any combination of the four. She will also answer to Miss Peggy, Peg, Mother, Mom, and Gran—a collection of names used by her sister, her in-laws, her children, her grandchildren, and her friends—all of whom have come to love her. There is no other category with Miss Peggy—the only people who do not love her are the ones who have not yet met her.

This is only some of her story. It is certainly not her life's story, it is the story of the beginning of the end of her life.

This part of her story is a part in which Miss Peggy has been a champ, though by the time some of you read this, she will likely no longer know that she has been such a champ, no matter how often we try to tell her. She may not even recognize those who have been walking alongside her for many years. She may not even remember that this story was told, or that she wanted it to be told.

"You are going to write about this, aren't you?" she asked one day while we were out for a walk. We had been talking about her sons and her daughter and how the gathering up around her in the previous few weeks and months had drawn her children closer to one another. Her children are separated by some twenty years from oldest to youngest, by the fact that they live in four cities spread across three different states, and by their having chosen to make their lives and their livings in very different ways. We are not the only crowd of children for whom such things are true.

We gently told her that the story of these days of growing darkness in her life was a story that belonged to her and no one else.

"You have to tell it for me," she said. "If we can, we ought to try and help some of those old folks."

To this day it is hard to know whether she was giving a permission or making an assignment. Miss Peggy has always been tricky that way; most mothers are.

For those of us who love her, the pages that follow are not our favorite part of her story. But it is a part of her story which has made us very proud of her.

It is a part of her story that is not easy to tell, for many reasons.

The emotional difficulty is obvious.

Chronologically, the struggle came with recording so many things happening at once over the space of a few short weeks and months; bits and pieces of the story had to be compressed in order to make the telling make any sense at all.

Technically, the telling is difficult as well. We are not professionals caring for a patient; we do not know all the language of professionals nor have we run this course time and again. We are just a crowd of folks who love Miss Peggy and set out to do the best we could to help her move to a new place, help manage her affairs, and help one another along the way.

We do not know exactly where her dementia will lead. Is it solely dementia? Is it going to lead to Alzheimer's? Can it be slowed or turned around? No one knows at this stage, not even the professionals.

However, she said this story was to be told, and so it shall be.

Looking back, it seems as though all of the conversations among the siblings and Miss Peggy were held and the plans put into motion within a few short weeks. It seems as though the whole thing moved very fast. It is not true, really. It took a while for the choices to become clear, to have a quorum of concerned children who knew it was time to recognize the truth about their mother, to talk straight with one another and with her, and to begin to figure out how to take the steps that needed to be taken in order to care for her.

It took us a while to find and do our parts—individually and collectively. But we finally took the first steps, and sometimes first steps are always the hardest ones.

One of the earliest memories of Miss Peggy we have is from the back seat of a Ford Galaxy on a Friday afternoon. Her first two sons were the witnesses, old enough to remember.

We two brothers, the oldest of her children, do not know why these particular weekends were chosen, we were too young to be invited to the family planning meetings. Whatever the adult criteria were, on certain weekends, the four of us would pile into the Galaxy and head north and east to the beach at Daytona.

Those were the days we learned to love the sea and the shore and learned some of the ways of both.

When we set off to Daytona, Dad would be behind the wheel, Mother would be at the other end of the long bench seat of a 1950-something Ford. The two brothers would play in a large sort of "playroom" Dad made by putting suitcases and pillows in the backseat floorboards to a level equaling the seat, and covering the whole business with two or three layers of quilts. Car seats and seat belts were years away.

Our father was pastor of a small church in Orlando in those days. In order to make ends meet, he was a PE teacher at a local high school, a school bus driver, and a day laborer on a construction crew. Our father was also helping to raise young children, raise enough money to keep the small church going, raise his own understanding of what it meant to be a pastor and a preacher, and raise his own sense of self.

For much of that time, the house that our homemaker mother made was comprised of four small rooms in the back of the church. There was a kitchen, bathroom, and two bedrooms. The congregation entered our house through a door to the left of the chancel. Church school classes were held in the kitchen and the bedrooms of our *house* on Sundays, as was vacation Bible school in summer.

While Dad would drive, we boys would roughhouse around enough to get in trouble and then be directed to lie still. Mother would lead the songs and hand out the snacks and declare the winner in the "count the cows" game. Sometimes we would nap in order not to get in more trouble. How much trouble could there be? It was only sixty miles.

There was always a moment in the ride to Daytona, to the sea, to the shore, whether the day be sunny and warm or rainy and cold, which it was sometimes, when we would begin to cross a certain set of rolling hills just a few minutes away from the beach itself.

Mother would always be sure to wake us up so we could be on our knees in the back seat and leaning over our folks' shoulders before we got to those hills.

The game was on, the game to see who could be the first one to see the ocean.

One of us would shout out that we could see it. Sometimes we could see it, sometimes we just wanted to win.

"I see the water, I see the water," she would sing when we could all see the shore. And we would sing along.

One of our favorite photographs of Miss Peggy was snapped while she was sitting on a beach along the Gulf of Mexico. A good friend had taken her there to rest and recover after a particularly trying time in her life, some four decades after our visit-Daytona-Beach days.

It was a cool day, she had on long pants and a sweater and a hat pulled down tight. She is looking out to sea. It looks to be late in the day but that could just be poetic license talking.

We all can remember sitting with her on one beach or another, staring out to sea at the end of the day, when it is almost time to head for the house and clean up for supper, the time of day when no one wants to admit that the day is coming to a close.

When you sit on the shore looking out to sea, you can sometimes see a storm far off on the horizon. You cannot always tell when it will come ashore—two days, two hours, who knows? You just know that it will come ashore, sooner or later. You look out across the sea and you see the gray patches that say that heavy weather is on its way.

The darkness and the rain will come. And there is no way to avoid it.

In the days when we all began to do the work to be done in order to move Miss Peggy, in the days when the diagnosis of dementia was first made, in the days when we learned to say the word out loud to one another, Miss Peggy would ask a lot of questions. A lot of those questions did not have easy answers.

But everyone my age forgets things, don't they?
Isn't there some medicine that can help?
I had a good day yesterday, I think I am getting a lot better,
*   don't you?*
You do know I could not bear to move to a home, don't you?

In a way, Peggy had been sitting on the beach in the evening sun for some time now. An old beach hand, she knew better than any of us that there was a storm coming ashore, a storm that would wash away all of her memories. She did not know exactly what language to use to describe it, but she knew it was coming. She knew it long before we did. And she was fighting it as best she could.

And she still is.

If you call her on the phone, she answers with some funny line. If you show up at her door, she has a wisecrack prepared for when she opens it.

If you take her for a drive, she goes out of her way to point out new buildings and things that are in bloom, even if the buildings have been there for years and the blossoms have faded. If she read the sports section that morning she will always ask how the Titans are doing or what we are to make of Vanderbilt's new coach.

But she knows, she still knows the storm is coming. She knows her world is shrinking, that a kind of darkness will be soon upon her, and it will be sooner rather than later.

She is sitting on the shore, and she can see the gathering clouds more clearly than any of us.

The front edge of the storm that is taking away her memory is now very close. And she, bless her sweet heart, can already feel the mist on her face. Those of us who know her the best and love her the most, those of us who take care of her business and tend to her care are beginning to smell the coming rain and feel the freshening breeze ourselves.

We who love her hope against hope that the storm will somehow move back out to sea, even though we know it will not. We are very afraid for her, and we cannot even begin to imagine how terrifying this change must be to her, no matter how bravely she faces it.

While we were moving Miss Peggy, we learned some new lessons about the woman we love. We learned things about how to care for her in this new world, how to face the dark of the future, and how to fall in love again with our family as we began this new and difficult journey.

The story of Miss Peggy is not ended, but the story of moving her is done. The time to tell that story is now, before the storm sets in completely and takes her away from us and from her own sweet self.

"I see the water, I see the water," she used to sing with her children to celebrate that the beloved shoreline was just in sight.

"I see the storm, I see the storm," is the new verse. The time had come for her children to all sing it along with her.

2

The Legend

The ordinary of life had become difficult for Miss Peggy. But she was as good at hiding her struggles as some of the rest of us can be at hiding ours. Knowing her history, adaptability, and her shiny entrance into any social situation, we should have taken keener notice of the signs. But they were signs her adaptability and independence taught her to hide.

In the summers in the South in the early 1940s when she was very young, Mother worked at the nursing home her grandmother ran in Roanoke, Virginia. She has told us stories about serving tea and lemonade to old ladies sitting on wicker settees on the porches lined with pots of red geraniums. There are photographs of her in pigtails and a cotton dress with puffed sleeves. She wore Mary Janes with white ankle socks trimmed with lace.

She says that is where she learned to be a hostess and to take care of folks. She could not have been more than eight or nine at the time.

These were also the days when her parents and two of their friends had an hour-long music show each week on a local radio station. She sat with dolls and coloring books on a couch in the hallway, watching through the big window into the studio where they performed, listening to them on the big speakers overhead.

Peggy was only seventeen years old when she married and eighteen when the first of her five children was born.

Our father was a pastor and later a publisher and then a well-known writer and speaker.

During the seminary days, she put her first two children in a grocery cart and hauled them to the laundromat and back.

When our father was a young pastor, she played piano in the services and taught Sunday school. When vacation Bible school came, she was in charge of the crafts. And hers was the first pot on the table at the potluck suppers.

When we moved to Nashville (home for both Mom and Dad) she settled into the life of a homemaker, a life that included being mother to five children, being the wife of an often on-the-road speaker, and being the chief hostess for a publishing executive. That life lasted some twenty years, some fifteen of which our father fought cancer off and on.

While he was a music publisher, she threw parties and entertained recording artists and singers who came through town and stayed in our house.

During the weeks the children got to go with Dad on the road, she packed a suitcase full of home: pictures and vases and napping blankets.

As years went by and our father made the transition from being a publisher to being a speaker and a writer, she traveled with him, charming the people who sat at the table with the wife of the shy speaker.

When our father declared that it was time to simplify their lives now that all but one of the children had left home, it fell to her to figure out a stylish way to go from a four-bedroom saltbox house in the suburbs to a two-bedroom condominium in the city.

For much of her adult life, she wore a lot of hats. Each morning came with a list whose execution called for a five o'clock start in the morning and most often led to a ten o'clock close at the end of the day—traveling, cooking, driving, shopping, hosting, dressing, decorating, entertaining, listening, cajoling, comforting.

But when our father passed away at a very young age in 1986, she had to start her life over again.

In the span of just a few months, her lifelong companion was gone, the last of her children left home, the condo became a solitary place, and her days became very empty.

She mourned. Rightly so. Her close friends drew closer. They took her to lunch, they took her to the beach, they took her in their arms.

Then one day she decided it was time to press on.

She sold the condo and found a new place to live. She wrote a book and traveled and spoke at retreats and conferences. In between bouts on the road, she worked as an interior decorator and as a florist, taking advantage of her way with making people feel at home.

She earned a specialized insurance license and then sold insurance for about twenty minutes. Her insurance career went by so fast that had she been a ballplayer people would say she had been to the major leagues for a cup of coffee and no more.

One day she was having a conversation with three of her good friends. These were the friends she made through the publishing years, years when the four husbands worked together. The crowd of them stayed in touch, included her in vacation plans, visited her when they came to town.

In the midst of the conversation the four women hatched a plan to write a book together about being friends through the ups and downs of life, about standing beside one another for decades no matter what happened.

The next thing you know Peggy had three books with her name on the cover, had gone on a book tour, and was speaking at retreats and conferences around the country. She was traveling so much that in trying to get her on the telephone we would discover she was on the back side of Texas or some other faraway place and would not be home for another few days, at least according to the publicist.

She would come home for a bit and tell us long stories about her travels and sing show tunes at the dinner table after dessert.

She was an independent woman, and we never worried about her at all. Her life was full and rich.

Eventually she came off the road and her life got much quieter. But we still thought of her as flying around the world.

"Do you remember when we used to go to the book convention in summers with your daddy?"

"Remember the first time we rode the ferry across to Nantucket?" she asked as though any of us who made the trip could have ever forgotten.

With a sigh one day—*"One day I probably am not going to be able to travel so much anymore, am I?"*

Her independence and the pride and comfort we took in it ended up sort of faking us out.

For a long time, the legend that was Miss Peggy kept us from seeing behind the curtain.

3

A Gathering Up

I n our family, being funny matters.

Funny is not a gift in our crowd, it is a calling. Prerequisite or responsibility may be more accurate terms. In our family, one's sense of humor may be different from the others, but everyone is required to have one, and to learn how to best use it. And because there are so many of us, we had to learn how to be fast as well as funny.

The house we grew up in had several core tenets. One of them, an adage my father used to repeat from time to time—"You only tease the ones you love." Being quick with a story, quick with a quip, and quick with a clever comeback were regarded among the highest of social arts.

Wherever two or three of us were gathered, someone was telling a funny story or someone was teasing one of the others. Someone was riffing on the stories or poking fun at one of the others or working on a clever comeback. And it all went pretty fast and still does. If you got the floor, you learned to hold on tight, it was only a temporary condition. Anyone can start a story, but in my family, it is the finish that counts.

Mother once told someone that one of her sons would interrupt himself if he thought he had a line that would get a laugh. She jumped over one of his punch lines when she said it.

Peggy is as bad as the rest of us.

One of the markers in the story of moving Miss Peggy is to tell of the spring night that a crowd of us were sitting around her living room laughing, laughing until we were crying.

We have been doing a fair amount of both ever since.

Our brother Michael called to say he had to go to Alabama to speak at a conference and thought he might come through

Nashville on his way home and maybe we should all meet and talk about Mother.

By *we*, he meant her four children.

Robert is the oldest, the writer who lives in town just a few minutes from Peggy. The rumors that he is the favorite child should be ignored, if for no other reason than the fact that he is the one who started them.

Michael is next, he lives in a college town some nine hours away, in Illinois, near a university for whom he worked for some years. He has spent his life in the work of the Church—as a pastor, an evangelist, a chaplain, and now an evangelist again—and he has a big heart and a great hug.

Sister, Leigh, is an artist who lives in Asheville, in the lovely mountains of North Carolina. She is pretty and funny and talented, and the three children she has raised reflect her art and wit and style.

The youngest is named Patrick. He lives a half hour south of the city and he is a print production wizard on the marketing side of a large book distribution house. He can sit down at the piano and play riffs that will make you weep, and he can laugh with such joy that you giggle days later just remembering his laugh.

By *worried*, Michael meant that he was beginning to notice the changes in her memory that all of us who love her had seen but did not want to really talk about.

By *getting together to talk*, he was hoping for a command performance, shall we say, a meeting where we would all come and sit down and talk about what was going on with Mother. Perhaps it might be time to make some decisions about how to care for her.

Time and distance had separated the four of us. No big battles, no animosity, no drama—we simply had grown our way into living different lives in different places. Our parents raised us to be our own people, and so we went off and did just that.

But it was clear to us all that we were sneaking up on the time for us to be the children who loved Miss Peggy in the sort of ways that we had learned from her when we were children and needed care from her. It was time to get started, whatever that might mean for all of us and our mother.

So we made a plan to all be together in a few weeks in Nashville. Mike and Leigh would come to town and stay over at Mom's, the rest of us would drive the few minutes to her place, and we would all sit down with her and have this very adult and very rational conversation about what needed to be done next. At least that was what we thought was going to happen.

Michael was a champ for calling the meeting, and it would have been great if he had shown up at the appointed time.

Michael rides motorcycles. Serious motorcycles, Harleys for crying out loud.

On the way south to Alabama, he had a motorcycle accident putting the aforementioned meeting in doubt. He was getting off the freeway in Memphis to find a place to spend the night, and a woman in an SUV failed to see him at the red light and hit him from behind and shoved him up underneath the vehicle in front of him.

He was fine, but the bike was totaled. Among other things, the bike being totaled redirected his travel plans. In a few days it became apparent that it was going to affect the big pow-wow.

He rented a car to get to Mobile to get to his work while the Harley folks got him a new bike. He drove back to Memphis, got his new bike and headed east to Nashville late on the afternoon of the *big* meeting.

He was in touch by phone off and on all day while he was traveling, and it began to be clear that he was not going to arrive until well past sundown, barely enough time for us to have a bite of supper together, much less figure out a way for the four of us to have a serious conversation about our mother's future. Furthermore, Michael's week had been more than a little exhausting and it seemed unfair to ask him to sit down and try to make sense of what was happening to Mother and what we all thought needed to be done next.

So even though Michael had called the meeting, the rest of us canceled the "big talk." Wives and children and assorted hangers-on were hastily invited and when everyone showed up, we did what needs to be done in such situations: we went to a local eatery, occupied three large booths, and ate piles of food.

We moved back and forth between the booths, rotating around so that everyone got to be with a different crowd every few minutes. Everyone got to be with Peggy for a bit as well. The matriarch is not required to change tables when the rest of us do. No talk about the big stuff we were going to talk about, just laughter and stories and catching up on the news.

When the supper was over, we took Peggy back to her house.

It was late and there was no longer any notion of there being some sort of big family conference about Mom's future. So we just sat in her front parlor and told more stories, both old and new, and teased each other and laughed until we cried great tears of joy. There was quite a bit of lying on one's back and kicking one's feet and pounding on the furniture that went with it. It went on for a couple of hours.

The four of us had not been together like that for years. We had forgotten how much fun it had been and still was to be a child of Bob and Peggy. For those moments the years and the miles that had pulled us apart seemed to slip away.

But on this night Peggy just sat in the corner in a chair. She laughed when everyone else did, and she smiled over us all because she was glad we were all together, but she was a beat behind all night. She told no stories and she sang no songs and she jumped on no punch lines.

It was evident to all of us that the whole thing was simply too much for her. Too much noise, too many words, too many people, too much of everything.

"I know I asked this before," she asked someone, *"but tell me again why Gwen did not make the trip with Michael."*

"Who is that sitting in the corner?" she whispered. *"Oh, yes,"* when the reply came.

"Where is Michael going to stay the night?"

"Is Leigh going to sleep here?"

In the general joy of that night and in the clear light of the next day when Peggy's children met at a local restaurant for breakfast, some things were evident to us all.

The first was that she was terribly suspicious of not being invited to breakfast. She knew we were talking about her. Our "it will be easier for you not to have to cook for us all" explanation was pretty thin. So was the "we have not seen each other in a while" story.

But we knew it was time for us to make choices for her that none of us wanted to make, choices we had never even thought about having to make for her. And we wanted to make them together.

Another thing we knew was that we would do our best to find ways to take care of Miss Peggy. It meant that we had to meet together again soon. It meant some research had to be done and some information gathered up and some responsibilities handed out.

The other bit that was clear was that her children had fallen in love with one another again. We stumbled upon, reveled in, and enjoyed the heck out of the truth that we were funny, that we loved one another after all.

In the midst of the laughter, we could see in one another's eyes that we all could see that she could not live on her own anymore.

Whatever it took, it was time to help Miss Peggy move on to the next place, wherever it turned out to be.

And we could see that we were going to do it hand-in-hand with people we loved. There were going to be plenty of tears ahead, and some of them could, we hoped, be tears of joy.

4

A First Gift

Someone was going to have to help her with her money.

It turned out some good news landed upon us right away.

In the weeks and months before we had our laugh-on-the-floor moment and then the get-up-the-next-day-to-begin-the-hard-work moment, the youngest of Miss Peggy's children had already begun to do just that.

In the quiet way that Patrick goes about his life and days, when Mother had asked him to help, Patrick began to help her take care of her bills and manage her money and work her way through the piles of paper that came in the mail, piles of paper she was having more and more difficulty deciphering.

For some months, Patrick was driving the thirty miles to the city from his home each Thursday to take classes to prepare to earn his CPA. He made it a habit to come to town early or to stop by after class in order to visit Mom. He added the extra miles and extra hours to his class day so that he could see her; go through the pile of paper with her; throw away the junk mail that was confusing her; take the bills, bank statements, and other papers home with him; make sure the bills were paid; make the deposits; and make sure she had a little money in her pocket and an available balance in her credit card account.

Over time, he put all of her accounts online so that he could keep track of the whole of her business from his desk. He would check it every day to make sure everything was okay. When she was worried about something financial, she could call him and he would know the answer, or close to it. Along the way he had to call some creditors and make some arrangements. He had to have some hard conversations with some folks on her behalf.

Patrick never talked much about what he was doing for Mother. He just did the work, did it for months before all of us even knew. Somewhere along the line, he had to be in touch with one of us about a particular thing, and his secret accounting service was revealed.

When we finally heard about it, we asked him about it. "Aw, I'm just helping her out a little bit," he said. "It's not a big deal." Gratitude was the collective, and proper, response from the rest of us.

Who knows what mistakes she might have made had he not stepped in when he did?

Who knows how much anxiety he saved her? Who knows what grief might have been in store for her had she kept trying to sort out all of her business herself?

We all know people for whom wrestling with money and personal business affairs has been a lifelong source of anxiety. There are stories from Peggy's life as a young girl—some of which she has told, some of which we pieced together over the years—that tell us that she has been anxious about money almost her entire life.

This anguish with money is something she passed down. And most of her children grew up being afraid of almost all things financial and not always able to manage our affairs very well. For more than one of us, anything connected to account numbers and previous balances and long-term planning and credits and debits are not exactly in our wheelhouse.

But long before we actually moved Miss Peggy herself, Miss Peggy's business had been moved to the hands of someone who was willing to put their hands to work for her, to the hands of one of her own children.

Patrick's jumping in to do the work that had to be done was pure gift—not only to Miss Peggy but to the rest of her children.

The realization he had done so and would continue to do so meant that the rest of us were free—and called—to discover what we could best do for her.

"Don't we need to do something about the insurance today?" she would ask. *"Are they going to cut us off?"*

After a week or two without some basic necessity she would ask, *"Can I go to the store and buy a few things yet?"*

Someone would invite her to lunch and she would call one of us— *"Is it okay to go? Can I pay for my lunch?"*

Wherever two or three are gathered, according to scripture, the One Who Came will be among them.

The faith of our family—the faith of all of Miss Peggy's children, however each of us is living that faith out these days— would say that we believe, and God knows we hope, that such is still true when two or three of us are gathered up to make the next choices for our sweet mother.

In the age in which we live, it is rare for two or three siblings to be gathered up at all, and whenever they are, they are not together for very long. They all have lives to lead and they are very often lives that are led far apart from the others. And when they are together for the few brief moments each year, they end up living into and out of and up next to the particular role that goes back to when they were all very young. Very often, our current ways of dealing with one another goes back to the days before we even imagined a role we might play in the life of a parent who was beginning to fade from view.

Our parents were always proud of the fact they had raised a crowd of children who were not alike, not cookie-cutter children. We are very proud of it, too, but the call now was for us to marry our differences into something that could be of unified service for our mother.

Since Patrick is the youngest sibling, it seems obvious to invoke the ancient words about "a little child leading us."

But the truth of it is powerful—Patrick's gift for Mother gave the rest of us the notion that we were free to begin to discover, relearn perhaps, what sort of things Mother would come to count on from each of us when it became clear it was time to move Miss Peggy.

Peggy's children are a crowd of pastors and poets, painters and production folks, people whose chief tie is the home she helped make for us. There is some possibility that if we were strangers who lived down the block from one another we might never have become friends.

But we are the children of Peggy and Bob. And what we were taught was that when the hard times came, we would not be alone.

If we could each do what we do best, there might just be enough to go around to be all the things Miss Peggy might need her children to be for her.

Wherever two or three, or even four of us, were gathered, Someone More would be among us. And between us all, it just might be enough.

5

Of Keys and Burdens

Once Peggy's writing and speaking days had begun to wind down, she found clerical work in a dean's office at a local university. She worked a few days a week. She shared the job with a friend from her church, allowing her to work a few days and then go out on the road to speak for a few days.

Some weeks she worked a couple of days and then went to the beach with her best friend Barbara for a few days. The key axiom in the house we grew up in was "When the going got tough, the tough got going—preferably to the beach." Our mother is tough, and has the suntan to prove it.

Other times she went to visit Michael or Leigh or a friend for a few days and then went back to work at the end of the week.

It was impressive. Not the working part, anyone can work. Managing to get people to pay you for not even being there is the part that impressed us.

She was in her seventies by then, happy to be around young people on a regular basis, people who responded to the mother in her, one of the most essential parts of the essential Peggy. She was happy to have the work, have the bit of money that came with it, and have the place to belong.

Everyone in the administration knew her and loved her.

Our family has a deep history with the university.

Our great-grandfather was one of the six charter members of the religious denomination to which the university belongs. In the school's early days, Mother went to high school there, my father was a college student there when they met. Others of us either worked or went to college there or to one of the denomination's sister colleges. After our father retired from the publishing company, he became writer in residence there, a position connected to the chaplain's office. A person wandering around campus will meet up with buildings bearing our family name. Miss Peggy can introduce you to staircases and trees and steps all over campus and tell you stories that go with them. Some of the rest of us have our stories to tell about the same campus, but they will not be told here.

Peggy was proud of working there. Every young kid from somewhere far away from home for the first time who came in contact with her must have been grateful to stumble into someone who seemed like *Mother* and *Home* to them for even just a few moments.

The others in the dean's office were glad to have her there for the same reason.

Another sign of their affection for her came as they kept her on the payroll long past the time when she could do the work they were asking her to do. The nature of the tasks kept getting simpler and simpler, and she could not keep up.

The dean and officemates never seemed to tire of going around behind her and taking care of things, but they were in touch, letting us know of their concern for Miss Peggy and offering to help in any way.

The time finally came when her actual children had to say to her that she could not go to work there any more.

For most all her life, when daylight came, Miss Peggy had a long list of places to be and work to do each day. It was true in the days before our father was gone and the children moved away, and in many ways it was just as true afterward.

But the time had come to tell her that her days and her lists were about to become very different.

Though it was not the only difficulty Miss Peggy was having with her work, the most frightening part was how she was *getting* to work. She was driving her own automobile.

By now the friend with whom she shared the job was no longer working, and so four days a week, Peggy was rolling out onto the expressway to head to work and home again. An hour a day in rush-hour traffic, traveling by rote, not really aware of the traffic that was moving around her.

The thought of it frightened us all. We began to be afraid of the telephone call that might come someday. We were also afraid of trying to take the car away from her. Who would not be?

Somewhere there is an older parent who just called their children to say, "I think I would like to give up my car and the independence that goes with it. Would you come and pick the car up, please?" But I suspect such conversations do not happen very often.

One day Miss Peggy ended up in a parking lot about a mile beyond her house, and did not know where she was. It was a long time before she told anyone that story.

But eventually she did, and other stories she had not told got around to of the rest of us. She would tell one of us a driving story, making the child promise not to tell anyone else. So one of us knew about the day she went two or three exits too far and ended up in a strange parking lot instead of the one behind the building where she worked. Another of us had been told about her coming out of the store and not being able to find her car. She told one of us about making a wrong turn and going some ten or twelve miles in the dark past the entrance to her town home complex.

One at a time these stories made us just shake our heads and giggle a little bit about old people and how it was going to happen to us someday as well. But once we went from wondering about Mother on our own and actually comparing notes and stories with one another, the picture became clearer, and more frightening.

Her children agreed it was time—the final proof being that not one of us or anyone we knew was willing to get in the car with her behind the wheel. Her grandchildren loved to go places with her, but only if she would let them drive. Some one of the four of her children had to tell her, the question was who.

There was some discussion about drawing straws for the assignment, but we agreed that if any of the other three of us tried to talk her out of the car keys, she would likely say no and call our brother Michael and see if we could do such a thing. We decided to skip a step and elected him to be the voice. It was a unanimous voice vote, with one obvious abstention.

Fortunately, he agreed to be the one and to come to Nashville in a few days and do it face-to-face. The university was on break, and she would not be driving across town for a couple of weeks.

If you talk to Michael about why he is a pastor, he will talk to you about calling and commitment, about preaching and prophesying, about the Christ to whom he gave himself long ago, and the Church to which he has given his life and labors. All of the things he would tell you would be deep and rich and thoughtful and true.

There is another theory, another thing that he will not tell you.

Some of us believe that at least one of the reasons Michael is a pastor is because he has the heart of a pastor. He has the calm demeanor, the gentle voice, and the big bear hug to go with it. There are certainly other careers in which such a heart might be given away, but such a heart is essential in a good pastor. Which is something our brother Michael has become.

Over the course of the years, in the places where he has served, California to Colorado to Kansas to Tennessee to Illinois, and in the dozens of places where he has traveled as an evangelist, he has helped a world of people listen to their lives at a given moment in order to see more clearly what to do next.

In those last few weeks before we began to actually pack Miss Peggy up and move her, his heart and his gentle way of talking to her began to come into play. We came to count on him to help her come to grips with new things that were going to happen in her life, to hear what we were trying to say to her, and to trust us to do the right things for her. He seemed to always find the right words to persuade her that the next thing that had to be done was the right thing to do, not just for her family but for her own sweet self.

"But how will I get to work?" she asked, a question for which there was not a good answer.

"I can go to church on Sunday, can't I? There is not so much traffic on Sundays. Won't that be okay?"

"How will I get to the store or the doctor or the cleaners? Am I supposed to find someone to take me everywhere?"

"What if no one will come and pick me up for anything, and I just sit here and can never go anywhere again?"

It was just the two of them together on the night Michael took the keys away. They sat in her living room. The rest of us sat by our telephones waiting to hear how it went.

The conversation was not easy for either of them. The freedom to come and go as you please is no easy thing to surrender. The call to be the one to ask someone to do so is not an easy one to answer.

Michael told us later that after a lot of back and forth, he finally said to her the same things she had said to him when he was a teenager and had been caught driving recklessly. "You would never forgive yourself," she had told him, "if you hurt someone, and so you have to stop being reckless." To a woman who had a sister die in her arms as a result of being hit by a car, the word rang true.

She handed him the keys.

By then, we had been having conversations with the folks at the university for some time. They told us that they had been following her around for a while, finishing her work for her, making sure she made it back to the building when she was out on campus, watching to make sure she found her car in the parking lot.

We told them she could no longer drive to work and that she was worried about letting them down. They said they would keep her on for as long as she liked, a day or two a week, if she could find a way to get there. For a few weeks, one of us picked her up and dropped her off in the afternoons. Before long, she wanted one of us to tell them that she was not going to come in anymore. They came to see her and brought her gifts.

Giving up the automobile was hard for Miss Peggy. It meant her independence was gone.

Running errands, going out to eat, attending church, weekend trips, going to work—all of those things she had taken for granted all her life—now were all dependent on whether or not someone would take her.

Giving up the independence itself was hard for her, giving up the burden of it may well have been a gift.

6

Moving Days

The first hard steps had been taken—her children were on the same page about what was to come next, her car keys were safe in someone else's hands, and her path toward a new way of living had commenced.

A few weeks went by, a few weeks living in and out of the reality of Peggy not having work and not having a car.

Friends and grandchildren and children came and went on a regular basis. We took her places and ran her errands, we accompanied her to the doctor and to the dentist, to the store and to church.

Her neighbors would come and catch us when we were leaving her house and getting in our car. They would introduce themselves, sweet folks all, tell us how much they loved Miss Peggy and then ask if she was doing okay. Clear signs of their affection for her, and clear signs that some of her behavior around them had made them anxious for her.

They had noticed the garage door being left open at night and the trash cans not being returned to the garage after trash pickup day. Once she knocked on someone's door because she had lost her key, though the key was on the ring, she just could not remember which one it was.

She went through a couple of weeks when she decided not to run the water in the kitchen because she was convinced a pipe had broken in the cold of the winter. Two plumbers and one electrician later, it was clear that nothing was wrong with the sink or the disposal or the water pipes.

The following week we found dirty dishes in the cupboard, dishes having been set aside until the water was working again. The bathtub was kept full of water, just in case.

We had ducked it for as long as we could. It was time to tell Peggy she *had* to move to a place where she would no longer be on her own in the way she had been. She had to move to a place where there would be folks to help her every day with the every-day things of life.

In a way, it seems it moved very fast. All of the decisions were made, the conversations with Peggy were held, and the plans were put into motion within about seventy-two hours one weekend.

Sometimes, the time just comes, and one of us had to tell her this was the time. Once again the vote was near unanimous. Michael came to talk to her again, we sat by the phones again, thanking our lucky stars for having a pastor among us.

First, the townhouse had to be sold. It was actually a second attempt. The first attempt had been two years before.

Miss Peggy was living in a townhouse at the western edge of the city, far from everyone whom she knew and loved. Looking back, her decision to move so far away from us several years before was a sign of some sort, a sign that she was beginning to make choices for wrong reasons, a sign that she was beginning to not be able to manage her own life.

Her choice to move to the western edge of town took her away from the almost daily contact she had with those of us who lived in the city.

It was a sign we missed at the time.

Looking back it is clear that she was in the early stages of dementia and that the disease had begun to affect her decision-making. At the time, we were simply beginning to worry about her being so far away from the beaten paths that most of us trod. And we tried to get her to move closer.

We encouraged her to sell the place and move back into the neighborhood where she had lived before, a neighborhood closer to some of us, a neighborhood that would give her more contact with those of us who lived in town.

One of our friends in the neighborhood is a fine real estate agent, and she not only agreed to help Mother list her house but found her a new place to live just a few blocks from us. She made an arrangement with the owner to hold off on selling their place until Miss Peggy could sell hers.

We spent some days staging Miss Peggy's townhouse for sale and working our way through all of the paperwork and such that goes with trying to sell a place.

And two things became apparent during that first attempt to get her to move.

One was that the real estate market for properties like Mother's were in the midst of a downturn, and she could not get the price she wanted. It turns out she could have gotten the price she needed but not the price she wanted.

The second thing we began to see was that she was sandbagging the sale. She would not make the house available for visits for one reason or another. She would show up in the middle of a showing and tell people what was wrong with the house. She would resist all efforts to compromise on price to make it easier to sell. She never mistreated the real estate agent in any way—to this day she asks about her, and asks us to tell her hello—but she was never resolved to move in those days.

It seems clear she had already begun to fear that she would not be able to live on her own much longer. She had an inkling perhaps that the day would come when she would have to live in another sort of place. Her desire to put that moment off for as long as possible made her dig in her feet. She was afraid this would be the last place she would live on her own, and she did not want to let it go.

It seems clear, too, that some of her reticence to move came from a fear she would not have enough money for what came next. She kept trying to hold out for the maximum price long after it was clear that she was never going to get it. She was terribly afraid of not having enough money. It was a fear rooted deep in her childhood, deep in the financial struggles of her father. The fear was deepened by the early days of her life with our father, the seminary days, the pastoring days, the days when his business career was just beginning, the days of living on a shoestring.

The whole business should have taught us one of the first lessons to be learned about the advance of the disease itself. There is a sense of willfulness that shows up, a good thing. There is also an inability to make good choices, a thing that is not so good. We have learned that the disease begins to have control over you rather than you over it, makes you fight harder and choose less wisely.

The frustrating year we spent trying to sell her place the first time around made us nervous when it came time to try a second time. The first go-around had been somewhere between mistimed and misplayed. We had just been trying to get her to move to a place closer to those of us who could help her manage her life. Now that we were about to move her to assisted living, we were nervous about whether or not we could get her to move.

The first concern was to find someone she would trust to sell the place. Perhaps a real estate agent of her own choosing, not of ours, might make a difference.

Michael is friends with a woman from the church Mother has attended for all of her life in Nashville, a woman who is a real estate agent. He had even officiated at her wedding. Teresa was the choice, a very good choice.

In the difficult market at the time, any agent who would work to find a buyer was a good agent. And this agent was as hardworking as we had ever seen.

But the thing that was most important was that Mother trusted her. Whenever we started a sentence with "Teresa said," then it was true as far as Mother was concerned—whether the questions were about staging the house, changing the price, or negotiating the contract. Without Teresa, and my mother's trust in her, we might still be trying to move Miss Peggy.

It was one of the lessons we learned in the category of Peggy holding white-knuckle tight to the things she knows because new things were beginning to scare her. It was one of the ways she was trying to tell us that anything from the past is to be held tightly, anything new is to be feared.

Having an old friend from her church responsible for selling her house made it possible to actually go through with it.

"If I move, then at least no one will call you in the middle of the night to tell you they found me walking down the middle of the road, will they?" She was laughing when she asked.

"Do we know where I am going yet?"

"Once I am wherever it is that I am going, what if my friends won't come to see me?"

"You won't make me go to a place like that, will you?"

A few months after the townhouse was sold, she told us that she never really liked the place anyway and wished she had never moved there. The real estate agent who sold it to her in the first place was the daughter of an old family friend, and she did not want to disappoint her, so she bought the place and lived there for years even though she hated it. Leaving it made her nervous about the next place, but not brokenhearted about the last one.

It was not as though she had never moved before.

When she was a girl, she lived in Greensboro, North Carolina. Then Nashville. Then Atlanta. Then once more in Nashville.

After she married there were homes in Orlando, Kansas City, Modesto, and Orlando again. Then home again to Nashville and its neighborhoods—two homes in Inglewood, two homes in Hendersonville, a home in Brentwood, two condominiums in Green Hills, and a townhouse in Bellevue. Sixteen homes, maybe more, in some seventy-five years.

Until this very moment, no one ever considered Miss Peggy to be a nomad.

In one way, Miss Peggy's wandering days were over.

But in another way, her wandering days have just begun. She has begun to wander her way into a new life and will spend a portion of the rest of her life wandering and wondering her way along from day to day, singing more and more about the sea and the storm that is nearing the shore.

7

The Wizards

Miss Peggy has a sister. Her name is Bo.

The truth is that her name is something else but when the first of her nephews was very young he could not pronounce her actual name. When he tried to say it, it came out "Bo," and the name stuck. He can now pronounce her real name but when he does she does not answer to it. Like most of us, the full name was only used when she was in trouble, and so she learned to selectively not hear it when it was said. The fact that the name was garbled by the one of her nephews who grew up to be an

English major and a professional wordsmith only adds a Benson sort of teasing humor to the whole thing.

For some of us, Bo has always seemed more like our sister than our mother's sister. She is only five years older than the oldest of Miss Peggy's children and some of us grew up playing with her in the backyard and halls and rooms of my grandfather's house. No one has ever played *Nancy Drew, The Hardy Boys,* or *77 Sunset Strip* better than we did. We climbed the maple beside the porch, played checkers on the floor, and performed Christmas pageants at the top of the stairs. Some portion of WWII was fought in the hedges behind the house, and the Packers/Colts football rivalry was renewed in the side yard there, or as much as it could be renewed with only three of us playing touch football.

One of us will tell you that as shy as they are, they only have about eight friends in the world and Bo is two of them.

Bo played with some of us as we all grew up, babysat some of the rest of us and later worked with all the rest of us in the family publishing company.

She was an assistant to my Dad for a long time and then came to work with some of us in the marketing department as the company began to grow. After the company changed hands and all of the Bensons went away, she worked in the magazine business and then in insurance and meeting planning and finally in a legal firm that specialized in care for the elderly.

We were lucky that Bo was our aunt and lucky that she has loved us like a sister, but we are also very lucky that she happened to go to work for one of the leading specialists in the country. When it came time to figure out how to care for Miss Peggy, we ended up sitting down with some of the best folks you can sit down with.

If you cannot be good, be lucky. And we were. Bo would be the first to tell us so.

The next steps in the process of moving Miss Peggy brought three critical things. And none of them were things that any of us had a clue how to do.

Financial plans had to be made that took all of Mother's resources into account—what those resources were, how best to manage them, when to use them. All these things and many more like them had to be worked into a coherent plan for the rest of her days, however many of those days there turned out to be.

Necessary legal documents required to take care of her estate and of her wishes had to be thought through, discussed among us all, drawn up and signed. There needed to be wills, trusts, powers of attorney, a great stack of things. And they needed to be attended to while she could still weigh in on the discussions and give voice to her own sense of what she wanted to happen in a future that was becoming more and more difficult for her to understand.

And we had to find her a place to live. The reality was that her care was going to require more on a day-to-day basis than any of her children could provide. We had to start to consider the criteria for her care and the cost of it and a whole host of other factors that we had never even imagined we would have to think about.

Now it was time to sort through all of her papers and line her up for the move into the next place, into the next part of her life.

It would have been much more fun to just keep sitting on her living room floor from time to time and tell stories and laugh until we cried. It would also have been wrong for us to avoid the truth, some of it the very hard truth of what needed to be done in order to care for Miss Peggy. As sweet as our night of laughing together was, the time had come for us to get down to work, to do the hard things that came with our mother suffering from dementia and no longer being capable of managing her life.

Not knowing any of the answers to many of the new questions, we collectively raised our hand, so to speak—something it turns out that a lot of people are not willing to do. Because of Bo, we at least knew someone to turn to.

Enter Patrick once again, who was willing to face the zeroes and commas and contracts and policies and realities with a clear eye and a steady hand. He was the one of us who went through the safe-deposit boxes, the storage bins under the bed, and the file folders in the cabinet. The one who sorted and photocopied and punched holes and bound everything up into three-ring binders.

And then it was off to see the wizards—the elder care lawyers—carrying the boxes of binders.

When we sat down with the wizards we learned some important stuff pretty quick. And early on, it was stuff we might never have figured out until it was too late—for Miss Peggy or her children.

One was that the Medicaid and some of the other resources we were counting on for her long-term care were not going to be available for the first two to five years. We had thought, like we suspect that a lot of people do, that once we moved her to assisted living, Medicaid would help her from the very beginning. After all, she had been a part of the system all her life, and we thought that when she got to this part of her life Medicaid would do its part. Medicare has certainly done its part for her health care.

But when it comes to assisted living, and perhaps other similar arrangements, it turns out that the government needed to wait for five years to make sure Miss Peggy had not hidden money somewhere—gifts to children, assets in offshore accounts, automobiles in other people's names, and other such things—before Medicaid will do what it said it was going to do if you did what you said you were going to do. (Which does reinforce the notion of withholding one's taxes until we see what they are doing with the money. If they can wait, then why cannot we do the same? What's five years among friends?)

When we heard the Medicaid news we just wanted to lie down on the floor. We began to wonder if it might not be easier to just go ahead and mortgage our houses to take care of Miss Peggy.

Then we got some news, news good enough to not only make us get up off the floor but to make us laugh out loud. Because it was such a Miss Peggy thing.

While working in the florist shop, Peggy worked alongside a young woman who had aspirations for something better. The young woman hoped to become a professional of some sort, insurance, real estate, some such. Once the young woman earned her insurance license, she did what most freshly minted insurance people are taught to do: she went around to her family and friends and neighbors to try and sell them a policy. A nice person like Miss Peggy quickly moved to the top of the prospect list.

Peggy had been kind to this young woman when they worked together in the flower shop. The young woman remembered and came to see her. Those of us who know Peggy can see this taking place. She bought a policy to encourage the young woman, set it up on automatic draft, and promptly forgot about it altogether for a couple of decades. If she ever told anyone about it, no one remembers.

When the policy turned up in her papers, we showed it to the wizards we were working with and they explained that it would cover the gap between now and the time when Medicaid would kick in. We simply wept.

Then we laughed. It was so Peggy not to want to disappoint someone and have it turn out in her favor.

At the risk of sounding as though we are giving advice, we will say we believe these things are true when it comes to taking care of your parents, the things that we learned so that we are not still lying on the floor overwhelmed by the whole business.

Do not try this on your own. Go and find some professionals to help, a lot of the system is too complicated. Or at least too complicated for writers and preachers and artists and production whizzes. Some of the advice you hear will not be fun to hear. But hearing it sooner is better than hearing it later.

We walked away from the first wizard meeting certain they had saved us upwards of a quarter of a million dollars, money the family did not have then and probably could not come up with in the near future. Not because the professionals were tricky and we were not, but because they knew the rules and we did not.

We suggest that no matter how many notepads it takes, and we went through a few, it is a good idea to plot out the finances as soon as you can. There are ways that Medicare works and ways that insurance works, and a family needs to be out in front of those things. It is hard to do if you do not even make some notes.

No matter how old your parent is, run, do not walk, to an insurance professional and make arrangements for long-term care insurance, no matter who is going to pay for it. (Check florists to see if they recommend anybody. It's as good a place to start as any.) The good news about the modern medical world we live in is that most people are going to be around for a very long time. Such long life will be a cause for joy in many cases. The bad news about the modern medical world is that many of us are going to be around for a very long time, and it is going to cost money.

Get all the paperwork done as soon as you can. In Miss Peggy's case, it became apparent in a short time that we were right to have set up trusts, moved for powers of attorney, built our own relationships with her doctors, and arranged for living wills and such as quickly as we did. None of us wanted to admit it at the time, but she was not far from not being able to participate in those conversations. We were glad to have had them when we did so that she could let her voice be heard. And so that her children could all bear witness to her wishes.

"How long can I stay there before they will have to put me out on the street?" You are not going out on the street, Mom.

"You won't let them keep me around too long, will you? I do not want to embarrass anyone."

"Can we make sure that all of the grandchildren get a little something?"

Another thing we learned is this: We only have this one mom.

Doing this as right as we can is the task at hand. We will not get another chance.

The wizards taught us that the answer to all questions, in our case, was to choose whatever would make Miss Peggy happy. Anything else can be cleaned up later.

Thanks, Bo.

8

Pack It Up,
Move It Out

Miss Peggy agreed to move, and the serious packing began.

Her remaining stuff, only a small portion of which was going to make the journey with her, had to be sorted and packed.

But that was only the beginning.

When she began to pack herself up, she did not exactly know where she was going. What she and the rest of us did know was that she was going from a two-floor, two-thousand-square-foot town-home with a patio and a garage to a two-room apartment smaller than the bedroom of the place she was going to leave behind.

She was not only going to leave behind a fair amount of space, she was going to have to leave behind the china and crystal, the paintings and photographs, the couches and cushions, the baskets and books and all the other things that she had acquired in some seventy years.

When he was speaking, our father used to give a talk based on the scripture about building a foundation on rock instead of sand. Had he been around when we started to pack up Miss Peggy, he would have been giggling as we spent our days hauling away the sand of Miss Peggy's life. And he would have put his arms around our necks whenever he saw us weeping while hauling out the bits and pieces that felt a lot like rock.

Real estate agents will tell you that staging a house to sell means that a lot of favorite things have to go and they have to go now. By Thursday, say. Even if you are not sure where they are going to live next, they can no longer live in the house that is to be sold. Mother watched a lot of things she loved go out the garage door and into a truck to some unknown place.

Enter Leigh, who brought critical credentials to the table. One was that she had packed and moved a few times in her life and knew how to help Miss Peggy with that part when it was time.

There is a reason we Bensons know how to pack; we are gypsies by and large. Between parents and siblings, we have lived in many places, some of them more than once—Nashville, Greensboro, Atlanta, Roanoke, Asbury, Pasadena, Kansas City, Orlando, Modesto, Winter Park, Hendersonville, Brentwood, Green Hills, Hermitage, Bellevue, Los Angeles, Chicago, Naperville, Oklahoma City, Sacramento, Colorado Springs, Emporia, Springfield, Bourbannais, Barren Plains, Memphis, Cross Plains, Asheville, Emory, and Murfreesboro. When you add in the number of times some portion of us over two generations simply moved from one side of one of those towns to the other, we average out at about two states and a dozen zip codes apiece. Miss Peggy leads the way with nineteen homes as near as we can tell. But the rest of us are not far behind.

Nomad is evidently a trait one can pass on. We know how to pack it up and move it out.

In the beginning, Peggy packed as though she had to do it all herself.

For days and weeks on end, some portion of us would go to her place and try and help her organize. We would come in the door, swap hugs and greetings and news, and then she would launch into the day's apology.

"I am trying to get everything organized," she would say. "I need to get the closet sorted out."

"I am doing my best. I will get it done soon."

She would say these things as though she had something to prove.

She was trying to pack up things so that they would get to the right place, to the right person, to the one she wanted the things to go to. A chest of drawers for this grandchild, a pile of books for this daughter-in-law, and on and on.

Many nights she would be up all night—sorting out things, and marking them with handwritten notes on masking tape, and sorting them into boxes to be sure they went where she wanted them to go. She seemed determined to go neatly packed into her good night.

Eventually, she began to run out of gas.

Our sweet sister, Leigh, is an artist, an artist of quite a lot, one might say.

Some of her art is done with brushes and watercolors and cold-pressed paper. People pay her to paint portraits of their house because she can see something about them in the house that they cannot see themselves.

Some of her art is done backstage at a theatre company where she makes costumes and sets. They pay her for that too, though probably not as much as she is worth, as is true with most artists.

She has worked with children since her graduation from divinity school, in churches and other settings. She has raised three terribly interesting and artistic children. And she is in the top five of the quickest—read funniest—women we know.

A fair number of people who are not artists have the sense that many people who are artists are less concerned with organization and detail than, say, people who are bankers or accountants or other kinds of button-down professionals. Some of us fit the stereotype when it comes to certain parts of our lives. More than one of Peggy's children is perfectly willing to admit that there are huge swaths of day-to-day life in which it is apparent that organization and attention to detail are not among their weaknesses. At least two of us are nodding our heads just now, and one of them is Miss Leigh. (The other one knows who he is.)

But there is one thing true about artists and organization and detail: When it is time to perform, an artist throws herself into the work with both hands and both feet and all the love they can muster up in between.

Those are the moments when they spend whatever capacity they have for detail and organization. Some people call it rising to the occasion, others call it rising up on tiptoes to dance when the music has begun. To people who are not artists, the inability for an artist to focus on the ordinary detail of life can be maddening. But to an artist, it is merely a question of where you are going to spend whatever amount of attention to detail and organization that you have. And the answer is that you spend it on the next artistic endeavor at hand.

It takes a certain set of gifts to keep ducks in the row week in and week out. It takes another set of gifts to get the ducks to dance when dancing is called for. And that is exactly what Leigh did when the time finally came to move Miss Peggy.

Sweet Leigh was able and willing to do things that others of us—read sons—would never have done or been able to do.

And she did it all with the grace and style and humor we have come to love in her.

Leigh helped us sons and brothers wrestle with what was to go with Peggy to the next place, what was to go to the children and grandchildren and friends, what was to go to the needy, and what was to go to the trash.

Miss Peggy trusted Miss Leigh in a way she would never have trusted any of the rest of us.

Peggy is a collector, shall we say.

She once was the queen of several thousand square feet full of antiques and books and china. Though she had been downsizing for a fairly long while, going from twenty-five-hundred square feet to six hundred square feet meant that a lot of stuff was going to have to go somewhere else. And some of it was stuff that she loved, as did the rest of us.

For years, her children and grandchildren have teased one another about who had the piece of masking tape with their name on it that was currently on the bottom of a given piece of furniture. And Peggy has always had her own ideas as well as to what should go to whom. But the day had finally come when some of her favorite things, and ours, were about to go and live somewhere else. Somewhere Peggy did not live. She would never see some of these things again, and we would never see her with them again. And the sorting was harder than one might think.

A legendary couch that had been in one or another of Miss Peggy's houses since the 1960s was being moved away. All of us had spent long afternoons napping on it as the years had gone by. All of us had teased about who might end up with it.

A big, clunky overstuffed chair and ottoman that Mother had used for most of the last decade or so to camp out in to read and to watch the television was off to a granddaughter's place.

A dozen or so dining room chairs that we and all her guests had sat in for dinner over the years were off south of town, except the two she was taking with her to the new place.

A painting we all loved had been earmarked by Peggy for a granddaughter, china had been set aside to go to Illinois to a newly married granddaughter, a favorite chest was headed to a grandchild in Carolina, a lamp to a grandson, everyday dishes for a grandchild setting up housekeeping for the first time.

And then there were the books and vases and decorative pieces to be divided up or set aside or given away.

Leigh sorted through clothing with Mom to decide which clothes should go with her to her new place and which clothes should be given away to folks who needed them. The two of them sat together for hours sorting paintings and books and furniture to be spread out among her children and grandchildren and friends. Leigh patiently resorted everything a time or two when Mother would wake up in the morning and want to start all over or change the labels.

Leigh told us things that Mother was worried about, things that Mom might never have told the rest of us. She knew that Leigh would understand and pass it on. Leigh knew when we were going too fast for Miss Peggy and needed to slow down just a bit. And Leigh knew when we needed to back off altogether for a few days to give Peggy time to be more comfortable with the loss she was living through.

You should have seen our sister spending patient days sorting through photographs and papers and pillows, dishes and door hangers, cards and casserole dishes.

And you should have seen Peggy's grandchildren showing up in the last days before she moved to her new place. They showed up to pack and haul, to sweep and clean, to get the place in shape again and again for showing by the real estate agent and for the takeover for the new owners.

It turned out all you had to do was call up the people who called her Gran, who caught the nomad gene from her as well. They knew exactly what to do to get her stuff packed up into a truck and headed down the road to the next place.

Great piles of things were hauled away to people she knew and loved and to others she will never know.

In the days when we were clearing the decks so her townhouse could be sold, it seemed like the work went on forever.

But the accumulated matter of decades disappeared in a matter of days. And if we think that is what it felt like to us, we can only imagine what it must have felt like to Miss Peggy.

"Did that table get in the car that is going to Carolina?"

"Nobody else took the couch before he got here, did they?"

"I wanted her to have the crystal, you know."

"Did she come and get a painting yet? I told her she could choose any of them she wanted."

"What will I do with the rest of it? I cannot take it all with me."

Somewhere toward the end of the long process of going through her things it became apparent that we were not only packing up Miss Peggy so she might head into her new life but that we were packing up a fair portion of our old life as well.

At some point, a moment will come when we are to be separated from most of the things that remind us of the places where we grew up, the things that meant home to us. Some of them we will help haul out the door so they can go home with ones who love us. Some of them will be carried away to strangers. Some of it has to be hauled to the trash.

Some of it will be sand, some of it rock, and some of it treasure. But all of it will be memories.

9

Homing In

We actually began to pack up Miss Peggy without really knowing where she was going to go and live. But we knew we were going to do our best to see that her last digs were as nice as they could be.

Miss Peggy did not always live in nice digs. We do not know much about the places she lived before she had children. She lived in places as a girl in Georgia and Virginia and Carolina, and the people who might tell us about them are gone, along with the stories we did not have the sense to ask for years ago when we met them on family vacations.

We do know that when our father was in seminary in Kansas City, she used to put her two young boys in a grocery cart along with the laundry and walk several blocks to the laundromat, which did give us one of the famous laugh lines in our family. Our father used to say that on weekends he would ask his bride if she wanted to go down the street and watch a few loads of wet wash go round. She always said yes. Romance is a lovely thing.

Some of our first memories of Miss Peggy's digs are of the rooms in the back of the church in Orlando. The next place we remember calling home was an apartment carved out of a basement garage in a 1950s tract house in East Nashville.

From there the small family went from one small rental place to another until we got to the big house our father designed and built for us in Hendersonville, Tennessee. It was the one with the five bedrooms and the balcony and the patios and four acres along the river. It is still the one we think of as the old home place, the one we still see in our minds each year when someone on the radio sings, "I'll Be Home for Christmas."

It is the place where we grew up thinking all of our days would be sunny and bright. Some of the time, we were right.

A lot of things changed once we got to that house on Bayshore Drive. The last of the siblings came along. Our father became a successful publisher and influential speaker and writer.

Even our vacations began to change.

Miss Peggy went from being willing to spend a few nights in a Coleman camper at a state park to preferring a small but comfortable house on Nantucket. Ever since those days, she has maintained that a Holiday Inn without a pool is as close to roughing it as she is willing to go. Not only had our father's fortunes improved, our mother's choice of accommodations rose as well.

Her children made the transition right along with her. One summer we were playing stickball with some kids in cut-off shorts at a state park outside Sparta, Tennessee, and before you knew it we were being served high tea at The Brown Hotel in London.

My father did the work to make the money to make these things happen. My mother was the one who dressed us up and taught us to travel in style.

When she would pack us all up for the road, every suitcase carried in it some bits and pieces of home she would pull out when we got where we were going. There were photographs and napping blankets and little books for the hotel coffee tables. There were vases from home—someone was dispatched to gather up flowers for each room. Some people unpack when they arrive at their destination, Miss Peggy was nesting. When you went on the road with Miss Peggy, you never really left home.

Helping her move to a place that would never feel like home—to her or to any of us—was never really in the cards.

When the search began for a new place for Miss Peggy, the first thing to know was what level of care was right for her, not only in the short term but in the long term as well. All assisted living places are not the same.

We are not professional health care folks, so it would be unwise to pretend we could explain the differences between independent living and assisted living and nursing home care and on and on.

What we can say with some confidence is that different folks need different levels of care. And since the first step—the move to an assisted living community—is the hardest, then it is important to be sure the first step is as right as it can be.

Whatever your Miss Peggy's name is, Mr. Paul, perhaps, the first choices are going to matter a lot.

Someone who suffers from dementia is about to slowly, surely begin to enter another world, a world they never imagined they might enter, a world without the things and patterns and people and daily life they have always known. For those called to care for them, the first call is for us to be as certain as we can be to help them arrive somewhere where they will be comfortable, where they will feel as much at home as is possible.

In the short term, they are likely to be less than thrilled, no matter what choice is made and no matter how much say they have in that choice. Those of us at their side are called to help them make a choice in the short term that will be best for them in the long run.

The professional advice we got was to determine the criteria that mattered the most—where there was a place close to those of us who would be seeing her the most, how many dollars the apartment was going to cost each month, how much space there was going to be, how comfortable she might be in it, what sort of care she needed in the short term, and whether they could provide the care she would need in the days to come.

But in the end—after going online and gathering up information, after driving the city and doing drive-bys and walk-throughs, after looking at floor plans and care plans and financial plans, we made a choice. We managed to manage the process, doing our best to make sure Miss Peggy was not too involved in the details of the search. If we had let her, she would have vetoed any place we showed her, simply because she did not really want to go in the first place. As it was it took her ten days and a half dozen visits for her to "approve" the place we found for her.

There is a very real possibility that the children of a Miss Peggy or a Mr. Paul may choose the wrong place. However, the odds are pretty good that their judgment is better than the judgment of one suffering from dementia.

Anyone responsible for making such choices for a parent works with a common set of criteria—affordability, location, cleanliness, services. The professionals we worked with gave us two other sets of criteria, which made all the difference for Miss Peggy and for those who love her.

The first set sounded like this: Can you see your mother living there? Can you see her sitting in the dining room, can you see her walking the halls? Is the apartment the kind of place where she can make a home? Does it look like a place she belongs?

The second set was like unto it: Can you see yourself going there to see her? Does the place look inviting enough to you so that you are willing to go in? Can you see it as your mother's new home? Will you go and see her there once she is, in fact, living there?

In the days after Mother gave up the keys to her car, the one of her children who could make a list and run an errand and haul Miss Peggy around from place to place was called for. Enter Robert.

He lives closer to her than any of the rest, and his skill set was perfectly matched to such tasks.

When it comes right down to it, he is a person who likes to make lists and check things off until everything is done. He likes it when the trains run on time and is willing to get up early and stay late if that will help them to do so.

He knows how to find professionals to help with the things the rest of us did not know how to get done and is unashamed to call them in no matter how simple the task. He knows how to call and ask questions of doctors and lawyers and to stay on the line until he gets someone to answer the question. He scheduled the rental trucks and organized the days for the move.

He knows how to show up and how to lift and how to tote. He is highly accomplished at the art of waking up in the middle of the night in a cold sweat about some bit of something that might have been forgotten.

And Robert became the one to find Miss Peggy a new place to live. The criteria were set and off he went around the city, looking for the place that seemed right for both Miss Peggy and those of us who would be the ones to go and see her.

One place made the most sense in terms of location but we did not even bother to get out of the car because the entire front stoop was the smoking deck. Four rocking chairs, two giant ashtrays, and a small door did not seem like the place for Miss Peggy at all. It did not even seem a likely place to spend the night had it been a motel on the interstate, much less a place to move someone you love.

Then there was the place we visited one day in a driving rainstorm. Visitors parking being a hundred yards from the front door did not seem like a really good thing that day, or ever, when one lives in the subtropical South as we do.

In another place, we entered a lobby where we were greeted by a row of several oxygen tanks on rolling carts with dirty towels hanging from the handle bars. The receptionist did not greet us for ten minutes because she was busy talking to a fellow employee about the extra hours she was being asked to work on the weekend. This did not make us feel better either. But (and we offer this with far more sarcasm dripping from our voice than we are generally willing to admit) at least the person who was going to come and show us around the place did say through the speakerphone on the receptionist's desk that he did not have time to talk to anyone before lunch. Were we to hand our mother over to such people?

Then there was the place with the violins in the lobby. It is a beautiful place, in a lovely part of town. It felt pretentious though, maybe a place where a girl who used to haul her kids to the laundry in a grocery cart might not feel so comfortable. Not to mention the kids who used to get hauled in the cart, our trips to the harbor in Nantucket and to tea in London notwithstanding.

We expect these places do a lot of good work. We expect they take good care of the people who live there. And for every crowd of children who found these places somehow unsuitable, there are clearly dozens who found these places to be just what they were looking for.

And they are absolutely right. And so were we.

It was hard enough for us to move Miss Peggy to the likely last place she will ever call home. But it would have been unbearable to have chosen a place for her where she might be embarrassed to host her family and friends.

For it to be a place that none of us would be willing to visit her in the days when her life is disappearing would be just as bad.

In a general sort of way, the services are going to be the same from one place to another. So are the costs. They are all staffed by people who, bless them, have some sort of heart in them for others—the way pastors and schoolteachers and nurses and others have hearts for those who are in need. And legal requirements for care and treatment and attention come into play in all of the places.

Miss Peggy had to move somewhere. When you go to pick a place for such a woman to live out a new sort of life, a place that is likely to be the last place she will ever know, you do not pick a Holiday Inn without a pool.

We finally did find a fine place for Miss Peggy.

We knew it when we came around the corner of the drive and saw it for the first time.

Though it is the middle of the city, it looks a bit like a small resort hotel you stumble on in the mountains of Carolina, a place one would be glad to see after traveling all day in a crowded car, a home-away-from-home kind of place for however long the next season of the journey was to last. If you travel the road with Miss Peggy long enough, you get a notion of what sort of place will make her grin when you come around the bend.

It is a part of a campus of religious institutions, a place where you hardly ever visit without seeing a nun crossing the campus, a place where prayer has been soaked into the walls over the years.

It is a place where the people are kind and gentle, where they called her Miss Peggy from the very first day, as good Southerners should, where they know the names of those of us who come to see her, where they watch out for her and are in touch if something seems amiss.

In our minds' eyes, we can see her sitting on the porch watching and listening to the children at the playground across the way, we can see her walking through the lobby and down the hall, we can see her at the table in front of the fireplace in the dining room, we can see her in her small apartment looking to the sunrise out over the lawn.

And we can see ourselves turning the corner into the parking lot and going through the front door. We are comfortable in the halls there and can see ourselves in her apartment.

Our excitement in finding the place was genuine, and she could feel it. She felt it enough that it convinced her that she might come to call it her own.

"If Leigh and her girls come to visit, where will I put them?"

"What if I cannot afford it and they turn me out?"

"You do know that all of my things will not go in there, don't you?"

"Are they going to be mad at me if I do not go to Mass?"

"Will anybody ever come and see me here?"

If people come and visit Peggy in her new apartment and think only about the great houses where Peggy entertained them or presided over lovely dinner parties, then her new apartment does not look like much.

But if you know Miss Peggy at all, then you can see that the new place, the smaller world to which she has moved looks like it has always been a Miss Peggy apartment. Like a house at the shore or a hotel room on the road she turned into home for a crowd of us along the way, this place was just waiting for her to arrive. She worked hard, and so did the rest of us, to make sure that whoever you were, whenever you went in the door, you would not be surprised to find you are home at Miss Peggy's house.

One day her daughter-in-law, the one we call Miss Sara, came home after lunch with Miss Peggy and was telling about some of the new struggles that had begun to surface. And the stories she told made us sad. Sad enough to cry, truth be told. So we wept together.

At the end of the weeping, Miss Sara put her hands on her waist and looked in our eyes. "The trick," she said, "is to be sure to keep your eyes open enough to see the essential Peggy underneath all the rest." She was talking about something else altogether, but it is true of Peggy's new digs as well.

Peggy has a certain style, and no matter the size of the platform—from 600 square feet to 5,000 square feet and back to 600 square feet—you expect a Miss Peggy place when you walk into the place. It is about color and light, it is about decorative things and practical things, it is about little bits of art and glass, little photographs, the lamps on the shelves and the books they sit alongside. People hire people to do this for them. Not Miss Peggy—she is the one they hired over the years to do it for them.

When you come to see her, sit quietly for a minute—in the minutes after she greets you as though she has been expecting you for days—and then open your eyes slowly, and you can see what Miss Sara saw.

As expected, she brought a case or two of home with her. There are enough of her things that suggest something built on the rock upon which we were raised to steady us when we feel Peggy's whole world is on shifting sand.

And Robert helped her find and make a place where we can still catch a glimpse of the essential Peggy.

If you are a friend of hers, come and see. But come quickly. And look closely.

10

Small Prices

Miss Peggy is of the generation of women who go to a salon to get their hair done each week.

When we were growing up, she would head down the twelve or fifteen miles along Gallatin Road from Hendersonville to Madison to see Edna. Edna worked at a salon in a shopping center, and she did Miss Peggy's hair.

We learned over the years, Edna knew all of Miss Peggy's friends and virtually everyone else in the city. We learned this by going there with Miss Peggy to sit and wait while she got her hair done for Sunday church. Every child did not go with her every week, but we went often enough to learn to pay close attention to their talk.

The salon is where we first heard tales told by ladies who get their hair done each week. It is where we learned that secrets are things that you only tell one person at a time. It is where we learned to listen very carefully the first time a story was told because real ladies never repeat gossip.

When the Beatles changed the world, including the market for flattop haircuts, we got our hair cut in a Sir Paul McCartney kind of way by Miss Edna and fell in love with her at the same time. Everyone who ever saw Miss Edna in the sixties fell in love with her on the spot. Indeed, a country music star in our neighborhood was swept off his feet by her, and she was swept off to a life of what turned out to be no small amount of luxury. And some of us had to find someone else to cut our hair.

Now, we sometimes find ourselves spending an absolutely inordinate amount of time working our way through the logistics of transporting Miss Peggy to her favorite salon to get her hair done each week. If you had told some of us that there was a moment in our future when we would spend a couple of hours each week making arrangements for Peggy's trips to the salon we would have laughed out loud. We are laughing no longer.

Barbara is the still-living and yet somehow already sainted best friend of Miss Peggy. They have been going to the salon together for years. Most weeks, Barbara makes the appointments for them both at their favorite salon and goes by to pick Peggy up.

Miss Peggy has other really good friends. There are the ones who come and take her to lunch every month to celebrate someone's birthday. There are only four of them who ever go to the birthday lunch, so how they end up needing a birthday lunch once a month is beyond us. Arithmetic is not important in the group anyway; they will not say how old they are.

There are also Miss Peggy's dear church friends, the ones who call her on the telephone and invite her to parties and sit next to her when she goes to church.

But Barbara is a friend to her like no other. Even so, circumstances intervene sometimes, and Barbara cannot take Peggy to get her hair done. Barbara has children and grandchildren spread across a couple of states, and from time to time she insists on seeing them. Of all the nerve.

Some of us muttered under our breath the few times it fell to us to figure out the salon logistics when Miss Barbara was out of town seeing her own grandchildren instead of making sure that our mother got her hair done.

Those are the weeks when the quest for a hair appointment and transportation to and from becomes a major thing. We still look at ourselves in the mirror from time to time and wonder what it is about the choices we made early in our lives that we have been reduced to making hair appointments for old ladies.

For a New York minute we tried to get her go to another place on another day in the name of convenience.

After a few weeks we began to understand that getting her hair done when and where she wanted to was about more than just getting her hair done.

If you are the one who goes to get her groceries each week, she insists that the bananas be green, the oranges be no larger than a baseball, the cottage cheese be small curd and 2 percent fat.

If you bring her a latte when you come to call, she likes the medium size, she likes it poured into one of her nice cups, and she expects you to sit in the chair on the right and not the left.

There is a preferred pain reliever and a particular size for a carton of milk.

If you take her to the doctor, she wants to be in her car and not yours. If you say you cannot take care of something on Tuesday, but can on Thursday, she will call someone else and get them to do it on the day she wants it done.

"You know you cannot get tangerines at our store?" she asks, though she has not been in the store in months.

"Do you know what this means?" she asks, looking at a bill. *"Are they going to cut off my telephone?"*

"If I go to dinner with her, will she bring me home, or do I have to stay at her house?"

"Will I be in trouble if I did not give the right time for when I was coming back?"

"You do know they have been going through my apartment while I am away, don't you?"

All of these things are a sign of something larger. They are symptoms, in a way. They point the way to another truth. All of these things are about her having some bit of control over a life that is reeling more and more out of her control every day.

Miss Peggy has very little in her life that is left under her control. She is not allowed to drive, which means she is not allowed to go wherever she wants whenever she wants to go there.

She has to sign in and out of her building, which means she cannot even take a walk without someone keeping tabs on her or accompanying her.

Someone else pays her bills, takes care of her taxes, and makes her bed. Someone else dusts her shelves, someone else picks up the little bit of groceries she now takes in, someone else gets her dry cleaning done.

Someone else drives her to church, takes her to the doctor, cooks her meals, takes out her trash.

By Gumby, she is going to get her hair done every week, in the salon of her choice, if for no other reason than that she has very few choices left. Anyone who helps make the appointment and makes sure that she keeps it, anyone who picks her up and gets her there on time, anyone who sits alongside and chats up the hairdresser while she cutes up Miss Peggy is an enabler, to be sure. They are also a heroine.

The important thing is that they are enabling Miss Peggy to have some bit of control each week over a life that seems increasingly beyond her control.

It is a small price to pay, whether we are taking her to the salon or picking up her groceries or sorting her mail.

It will not be long before we will all wish we could pay such a price again and again, when we cannot.

11

Stay in Touch

Late one Saturday night, we got a telephone call from one of the grandchildren. They had been trying to reach Miss Peggy all day and had been unable to do so. They were worried.

We tried to call her as well. The call would immediately roll to voice mail. Leaving a message for Peggy is of no value because she has long since stopped retrieving voice mail. In fact, one of her daughters-in-law has now recorded a message that goes something like this—"This is the voice of Peggy's voice mail. Peggy does not actually listen to her voice mail, and if you want to talk to her you will have to try back later on."

It turns out that the reason no one could reach her on her mobile phone was that she had set the charger down somewhere in her apartment a couple of days before. The somewhere was the corner of the closet where she hides her purse so that the folks trying to get in from the roof will not find it if they get into her apartment. Once the battery ran down, she was cut off from the outside world.

On the weekends, if we call her building we get an answering service. And it can be a bit before we hear back from one of the staff, which is perfectly understandable. But it is also unsettling, our having just the one mama and all.

After a bit, we heard back from the caregivers, everything was fine, though they could not find her phone.

A couple of days later we had a land line installed, with a telephone in both rooms, not a portable one that could she set down long enough for the battery to run down but one of the old-fashioned kind that was powered by the phone connection. And we did not show her how to turn the ringer off.

It was such a simple thing, an obvious thing. But it means that she can always find one of us and be found by one of us. Or at least during those times we know she is supposed to be there.

When someone suffers from dementia, a lot of the practical little things can become difficult pretty quickly.

Peggy can open her mailbox downstairs, take out half her mail, forget the other half, leave the key in the box and go back upstairs and not be able to get into her apartment because her key is downstairs, and she has no idea where it is.

She can head downstairs for her regular physical therapy class and cannot remember which of the three floors it is on.

She will meet us at the door and tell us she cannot find the car key, the one we keep in a box where it is always kept, so that when one of us takes her somewhere she can ride in her own car. We open the box and there it is.

A telephone number that has been the same for decades and locked in her memory for all that time is suddenly lost.

Her proper schoolgirl handwriting loses its lines and she cannot read her own notes to herself.

A moment comes when someone has to think through all sorts of little steps that we never thought we would ever have to do for the one who taught us to do many of them in the first place.

We discovered that in moving Miss Peggy, we were going to have to go more than a few steps beyond just unpacking her.

It should not be a surprise, but it did take us a little while to figure out one simple solution to the confusions in her new life.

First, we changed the mailing addresses with all of her business accounts. Unless it is marketing mail, which is impossible to stop, she now gets no mail with numbers in it. No bills, no numbers, no anxiety, no panic. Anything with numbers—insurance, credit cards, Medicare, doctors, and so on—goes to one of the other of us, the ones who are to take care of those things for her.

What she gets in the mail now is the odd promotional brochure, the stray marketing ploy, and, best of all, cards and letters from people who love her.

We cannot—thanks be to God—keep people from repairing the roof over her head, from making her bed, dusting her shelves, or taking out her trash, from making sure she is up and dressed and taking her meals, but we have learned to manage as much as we can so that her days are not filled with anxiety about things that can be managed by those who love her.

Along the way we began to hear Miss Peggy ask when one or the other of us was coming to see her.

Anyone who suffers from dementia has a moment in the morning when they have to figure out who they are and where they are and what it is they are supposed to do next.

It became clear she was having trouble knowing which day it was, and she clearly was not able to remember many things from one week to the next. It did begin to make a difference if she knew it was Tuesday. If she knew it was Tuesday, she knew who was coming to see her that day. But a calendar became a larger challenge than she could handle.

For some weeks, before she moved, one of us would drop by to mark things on her month-at-a-glance calendar, the same calendar she had used all her life. She told us one day she needed a new calendar because the one she had did not work. She could not tell if it was Wednesday or Thursday. "Am I supposed to read it up and down or side to side?" she asked.

Over the months, we bought a lot of different calendars to try and help. A month a page, a week a page, a day a page, big print, small print, pencil friendly, ink only, plastic susceptible to sharpies only—as time went by, it was clear that none of them made any difference.

One day she would make three different appointments on the same day with three different people at the same time. Another she would book yesterday's doctor's visit for today because she had some memory of having been to the doctor in the not too distant past.

One day she would not know what month it was. Pretty soon she would not know what day it was.

One day one of us called to say they were on their way to take her to the doctor, only to discover she had been sitting downstairs for three hours waiting on us to arrive. She did not have time for breakfast, she said, because she had been sitting in the lobby waiting for us.

We had to get used to the fact that evidently there is a day out there when the days and the hours all begin to roll into each other.

And we would have to find a new way for her to learn to tell them apart.

As a last resort, one of us would go each week to print out a list for her for a week at a time. She would make plans for a particular day and not tell anyone or not remember she had talked to someone and made a plan.

Finally we took the calendars and the lists away and bought her a clock that only tells her what day of the week it is.

It is true that keeping Miss Peggy moving along is helped by her knowing which day it is and who is coming to do the things with her that we do each week. It also helps her to know that she will be on her own for the day and not have to dress up or take visitors or leave the building.

One day one of us comes to take her for a coffee on a particular day each week. Another day one of us comes to help her run whatever errands need to be run. There is a day when one of us comes to help her with her bills and other business things. A day is set aside for her to get her hair done. There are times for physical therapy and a day when she goes to a group meeting where she talks with other folks in the place who are also trying to get accustomed to this new way of living.

There is a day when one of us comes to bring her a latte from a shop around the corner, and another day that is the designated go-to-the-doctor day, and a day when a good grandson takes her to church.

And in between all of those regular sorts of things, people who love her and want to be with her call her to make a plan about some thing or another. Thanks be to God.

The difficulty is that she cannot manage the traffic of it.

Miss Sara is the woman who is kind enough to make a home and life and a marriage with the writer of this book. She has stolen, or at least adopted, his heart and may well be stuck with it until the end. And Sara loves Miss Peggy.

In relative terms, the two of them have known each other not anywhere near as long as some of the rest of us have known Peggy.

But they fell in love with each other early on in their relationship. Perhaps their mutual adoration for Peggy's firstborn son had something to do with that I cannot say.

She sees Miss Peggy once a week or so. They go for lunch or they go for coffee, they go to the movies or they go shopping or they go for things at the drugstore that Miss Peggy does not want to go and buy with sons looking over her shoulder.

And it was Miss Sara who set up a Facebook page for Miss Peggy so that those of us who love her and see her can keep up with her schedule since she can no longer do so for herself.

The Page helps us to keep in touch with one another as to schedules and such. Some of us are on the road sometimes and need to let the others know we are out of pocket in case Mother cannot find us and gets worried. Sometimes we have been with Miss Peggy and have discovered something has happened in her life that we think the others should know. Sometimes there is news from another part of the family we want others to know before Miss Peggy knows because she does not always get the details right when she goes to pass on the story. If we know the truth, we can share her joy or allay her fears or clear her confusion. The Page becomes a way for her children to be together. Something she would like, even though she does not understand how it works.

Her actual connection to her Page is the occasional visit to the second-floor library in her apartment building where there is WiFi, and we show her the pictures people are posting on her Page.

"Did you call me?" she will say when she calls you out of the blue.

"Do we still have the car key?"

"Can you print those pictures out so I can remember them?"

"Is someone coming to see me today? Is there something I am supposed to do?"

"Nobody needs me anymore, do they?"

It is a difficult moment when you realize that someone who raised you, cared for you, cheered for you, stood by you in moments both large and small in your life, someone who once seemed to hold the whole world in her hands now does not know the day of the week, cannot make a list, or any of the other little things it takes to manage her life.

You have to learn to be realistic about finding new ways to be with her and to care for her. Even when all of us want it to be like it was before. Even when she wants to pretend that all of this is temporary. Even when she says she is going to take her medicines and do her exercises and then she will be able to go home. Even when Sundays are "so quiet."

She is already home in some ways now, or as close to home yesterday as she will ever be again. Tomorrow she will be further away from the home she remembers and for which she longs.

Some of the first steps we took to move Miss Peggy were the hardest ones for us. We can only imagine how difficult they must have been for her.

These days, we take no small comfort in the courage she showed all the way along to her new place. We take no small consolation knowing we did everything we could to make her safe, give her a home.

12

Loss and Found

D ad was the king of the long, complicated trip—a ten-car camper caravan to Panama City at spring break, five weeks and five vehicles worth of folks to Canada one summer, a month in a house for a dozen people on Nantucket, fourteen of us (including two grandparents) traveling five European countries for four weeks, four rooms worth of family for a week at the annual publishing show—the list goes on.

Over time, Miss Peggy, who had inherited some pretty serious road genes from her father and mother, adapted quickly to life on the road with the traveling Benson show even as the names and vehicles and faces and venues changed.

When our father passed, she lost the love of her life. And she lost those great and happy adventures with him and the assorted hangers-on that made up the show. It was not the first of the great losses in her life, nor was it the last.

When she was fourteen, she and her younger sister were walking home from church on a Sunday morning. They were only a few dozen yards from home when a neighbor driving up the street reached into the back seat to help his child with something, and his car swerved in the direction of the two girls. Peggy grabbed Joan's hand and they ran toward the porch of the closest house trying to get away from the car, but they could not reach the porch in time.

When the emergency folks arrived, Joan was dead. Peggy was unconscious and hurt pretty bad. She woke up in the hospital the next day asking for her sister.

Peggy fell in love with our father when she was sixteen, married him when she was seventeen, had her first child when she was eighteen. In the end, there were five children, a big house along the river, a travel schedule that included a lot of fine places, and a set of good friends that included a fair amount of important people in religious music publishing.

The only thing wrong was my father's cancer. After fourteen years, he finally lost the struggle, and she lost the love of her life. He was fifty-six, she was fifty-two. Her oldest was thirty-four, her youngest was sixteen.

Miss Peggy's mother was never quite the same after Joan died.

For many years she retreated from the life that went on around her. In later years, she too began to suffer from dementia, and it seemed as though Peggy lost her mother all over again. Peggy's mother finally passed away in the early nineties, marking the third time my mother lost her mother. But she really lost her mother the same day she lost her sister.

Her father was next to go, some five years after her mother. He was the one from whom she learned the hospitality for which she was well-known. Neither he nor Peggy met a stranger in their entire lives. He was the one who supported our folks in their early seminary and pastoring years, years when they had a good deal less than one might have suspected from the generosity they showed.

And there was another of us, a brother named Tom, who was born between Leigh and Patrick. By the time it was time to move Miss Peggy, he had been gone for some years, having taken his own life in his early thirties.

Tom was bright and strong. It turned out though, to use Kavanaugh's great phrase, that he was too gentle to live among the wolves, and we lost him one dark spring night to a cruel death, a death that came from his own hand. He was the funniest of us all, and God knows we could have used his strong hands and his big grin and his sly humor as we rolled through the months we were moving Miss Peggy. It would have been easier, and better, had Tom been with us.

Those of us who were left went to work. Each of us doing what we could, sometimes doing what only we could do the best among the four of us.

But we went about the work knowing that there was more loss in store for Miss Peggy no matter what we did. At some point, she was going to lose even her memories of what she had lost.

She did not stop taking losses after our father died, but she did not stop traveling either.

The adventures changed. Trips to the beach with Barbara, trips to Europe with lifelong friends, visits to children who lived in other states.

When the signs became apparent that she was headed to assisted living, it also began to be apparent the traveling days were going to come to a close.

A farewell tour began to take shape.

Off she and her sister Bo went to Carolina to see Leigh and the grandchildren dug in there in the mountains. She heard her grandson's band, saw one granddaughter's college, saw the other granddaughter in a play, and charmed the whole crowd over dinner one night.

The next month, she went south to the beach in Alabama with a couple of her best friends from church. They walked the shore in the mornings and sat up talking and telling stories far into the night.

Then an invitation came for her to head north to Indiana to be with the three friends with whom she had written books and toured the country, and so she took them up on the invitation. There was great joy in the trip, but at the end of the trip, she too began have a sense that her traveling days were going to be over soon.

For years, she and Bo traveled to Illinois to Michael's house for Thanksgiving. So one last Thanksgiving trip was put together. Michael came and drove them north to spend the weekend with his family.

At Christmastime, Miss Peggy came to our house for the big feast, and then spent the eve of Christmas and the day itself with her sister, in keeping with tradition. All of us who were with her at the holiday were very aware of how hard it was for her to keep up.

She then went off to the beach with Barbara for a few days. As they rolled over the last big bridge before the beach comes into view, some of us suspect she was singing, "I see the water, I see the water." They had a sweet trip but it was the last one she's made.

"What if I do not take the right things to wear?"

"What if the nurses cannot find me downstairs for breakfast, won't they be mad at me?"

"Am I supposed to find us a place to stay?"

"Can you call them and tell them I don't think I can come?"

There were only a few more invitations for overnight stays or quick trips after that, usually from an old and dear friend. And one of us had to call for her and decline the invitation.

The farewell tour had come to a close. The adventure of the road had become another of her losses.

Thankfully, for her and for those who love her the most—children, grandchildren, her close traveling companions for years, her best friends from the church where she and my dad raised a family—we had managed to create one last memory of being with Miss Peggy in the places she liked to be the most, a kind of good-bye from her and a last memory for us.

Perhaps everybody ought to have a farewell tour of some kind. Perhaps it can make a certain kind of loss easier to begin to bear.

13

Going Out Singing

Paula, one of the people who takes care of Peggy was on the telephone. We were getting medicines lined up for a trip Peggy was about to take.

"Was your mom a professional singer or something?" Paula asked.

"No," I said, "why do you ask?"

"Shundra told me that Miss Peggy was singing to her the other night when she went in to give her the evening medicines. Something about Oklahoma, I think she said."

Mother's life has been a life full of music.

Her father studied to be a classical pianist, and though that dream did not come true for him, he was in love with music his entire life. He had a baby grand piano in the front parlor and a Hammond organ in the den. He was a church musician for almost his entire life and sometimes when you came to visit, he would be practicing on the organ. Sometimes he would have Bach or Mozart on the stereo, sometimes he would have the classical station on the radio. His house was where we first heard Broadway musicals, because he was playing *West Side Story* or *Porgy and Bess* while we played checkers on the floor.

Miss Peggy told us that on Saturdays, they would clean the house because her folks' friends would come for supper and cards in the evening. If you did your chores well, you got to sit with the grown-ups and watch them play cards and listen to them talk and laugh. It was the place to learn to be a grown-up. The music would play all day while you were working and all evening while you were watching.

There is a favorite story of hers that she tells, a story of she and Bo—those Siler Girls—singing duets at funerals.

And when our father was a young pastor, she played the piano in church on Sunday mornings. She was beside him for the whole life that he lived out as a music publisher and spent many a night and day in one concert hall or another or entertaining one artist or another in our home.

Miss Peggy has also had a show-tune reputation for years. A tune by Miss Peggy is kind of a must at all family gatherings, otherwise it is not much of an affair. At the merest of suggestions, she is more than happy to belt out "Everything's Up to Date in Kansas City." There are those who believe they have not actually had a party if they have not heard and seen her rendition of "I'm Just a Girl Who Can't Say No."

Music is not a foreign language to her.

There is another story Miss Peggy loves to tell. It's not about music but about moving into an aloneness in the world. It is about the day Peggy's firstborn got on his bike and headed out the driveway and up the street to his first day of school in Orlando. He was on his new red Schwinn, the one with saddle baskets, the one he had earned by giving up sucking his thumb so that he could go to first grade and not embarrass himself, and his mother, when nap time came.

He was headed to Killarney Elementary School, to Ms. Gillespie's class, and to a stellar first year that got him in the Bluebird group in the SRA reading program.

As Miss Peggy has told the story for lo these very many years, he rolled down the driveway and turned left toward the school. Miss Peggy was following him.

A few yards away from the house, he looked over his shoulder, and she was walking up the street behind him. "Go back, go back," he shouted to her, waving his arms furiously, hoping none of the other children in the neighborhood would see her. He was ready to be left alone to go into the world, we suppose.

These days, it is a little bit different. We keep—her children and grandchildren and all of us who really love her—keep following along behind her, and we keep wanting to say, "Come back, come back."

We think she would like to, but it is simply not going to happen.

"I am not ever going to get to go home, am I?" she said one day.

"This is home," we said. And it is true.

We are grateful we talked straight with one another about things we did not want to talk about in time to make a difference for the only mother we have.

We are grateful we each found a way to give back to her in our own way. The ways were different, but they were all important, and they all reminded us of the ways she had helped us to become the people we became.

We are grateful for the professionals who were ready and willing and able to help us as soon as we raised our hand.

We are grateful we ended up—all of us who love Miss Peggy— being able to hold one another tight and tell stories and laugh while we all traveled in the direction this disease can bring upon a family.

We are grateful for the courage Miss Peggy showed on the way into this new world and for the consolation of knowing we had done our best to help her to find a place to live in that new world.

We are grateful, too, for the things she taught us.

Things like "Always keep an eye out for the shoreline, even if you are headed into a storm. Always make home wherever you are, even if you are far away.

"And sing—always sing."

When we were by to see Miss Peggy the next day, we ran into Shundra in the hall.

"We heard Miss Peggy was singing for you."

Shundra grinned, her great grin, the grin that makes us certain that we are not the only ones who love Miss Peggy, the grin that lets us know she will be okay even when we are not there.

"She sang 'Oklahoma' for me," Shundra said. "It was great."

"Did she dance?"

"Oh, yeah," Shundra grinned. "She did the hand motions and everything."

Jackson Browne said something once in an interview that has come to mean much to some of us.

"Whatever optimism I possess," he wrote, "comes from knowing that new people are brought into the world all the time, and they come in singing." He was speaking of children, of course, and the way they bring joy into the world with them when they arrive.

Whatever optimism we have these days when we can see very clearly that Miss Peggy is moving out beyond us now comes from knowing that evidently people can go out singing as well. "I see the water. I see the water," she sings.

Hand motions and everything, no matter the storm that is coming ashore.

Notes and Acknowledgments

As is the case with any book, questions come up. Most of them go unanswered, writers have limited skills. I will do my best to answer some of them here.

There is a particular book we found to be very helpful: *The Thirty-Six Hour Day* by Nancy Mace and Peter Rabins. It was first given to me by my dear friend, The Jim Bailey, and I am grateful to him for the book and quite a bit more now that I think of it.

The epigraph is from a novel by Donna Leon. If you have not read her work, run, do not walk, to the place you buy books about Italian detectives in Venice. You will find a whole world there, and you will find something about yourself there as well.

The wizards are Tim Takacs and the other talented folks who work at Elder Law Care in Hendersonville, Tennessee. They are nationally known and ridiculously helpful. If you would like to be in touch with them, this is how you do so: 615.824.2571 or www.tn-elderlaw.com. Just so you know, these are people who will steer you in the direction of someone else if that someone else might better serve you. They are also very encouraging about the government websites because their experience is that the information is unbiased.

They suggest you take advantage of the wisdom to be found in, at, and around:

The Merck Manual of Health & Aging

The National Institutes of Health—nih.gov

U.S. Administration on Aging—aoa.gov

Medicare.gov

Administration for Community Living—www.hhs.gov/acl/

Clearing House for Longterm Health:

   www.longtermcare.gov

The publishing folks at Abingdon include old friends to whom I am very grateful for new chances—Pamela, Tamara, and their friends. And the divine Ms. Lil—I hope to never have to try to make a book that matters to me without her help.

Lastly, which is the absolute worst word for this—thank you to Sara, Michael, Leigh, Patrick, Barbara, J. B., Jimmy, Teresa, Jim, Dane, Shundra, Paula, Jessica, Bo, and the others who have kindly held my hand and listened to me as I wandered the path that led to this story Miss Peggy wanted to be told.

Namaste.

R. Benson

Sunnyside, September 2012

Robert Benson can be reached through his website at

www.robertbensonwriter.com/

or by sending a note to him at

1001 Halcyon Avenue

Nashville, Tennessee 37204